Sally Blythe is a psychologist and author who spent more than twenty-five years working alongside her late husband developing a method of assessment and intervention to help children who are under-achieving.

As both colleague and spouse, theirs was an extraordinary relationship, sometimes described by Sally as the most unlikely but remarkably successful love affair that lasted throughout their life together.

Some years after the husband's death she moved to North Wales where she continues to write and work. She has three adult children from a former marriage and seven grandchildren.

To Carol, the hospice movement, my children, my sisters and Haydn.

Sally Blythe

Because You Were There

(2nd Edition)

Austin Macauley Publishers®
London • Cambridge • New York • Sharjah

All of the events in this memoir are true to the best of author's memory.

A CIP catalogue record for this title is available from the British Library.

ISBN 9781037121203 (Paperback)
ISBN 9781037121210 (ePub e-book)

www.austinmacauley.com

First Published 2026
Austin Macauley Publishers Ltd®
1 Canada Square
Canary Wharf
London
E14 5AA

Foreword to
Because You Were There

As I contemplate giving this collection of letters to the person who has acted as my counsellor for the past 9 months – since the death of my husband nearly a year ago – I question whether it is an act of supreme arrogance to think my story is different from that of anyone else who has had to traverse the journey of loss and bereavement.

I have learned that bereavement is never the same twice; that it is unique to the relationship which can no longer be in this world; that just as every life is unique, so too is loss – personal in its intensity and duration, shaped by its own colours, senses, feelings, and emotions, for grief is as deeply physical as it is emotional. It is the hidden sickness in our modern world – brushed under the carpet with comforting words in the first weeks, embarrassment in the weeks that follow and then the inevitable loneliness that is the journey that only the bereaved can travel – death and loss are too uncomfortable for people to talk about, and so we – who are left behind – enter uncharted territory without either map, compass or travelling companion.

Somewhere in my life I was given the gift of being able to write. Professionally, I have always stuck to logic and fact; it is so much easier, but in this – the most intense challenge of my life – I have been forced to face my own emotions, fears, desolation and the very first shoots of recovery. I am only at the beginning of my journey forward, but I hope that in describing some of the process I have been through in the first year after my husband's death, and sharing feelings that could never be talked about at the time, my story may be of help to others who are still overwhelmed by the early stages or episodes of grief, when I know I wondered if I was alone and would be alone forever.

There is progress, often three steps forward followed by two steps back, and I hope I never entirely forget, for grief is the other face of love and love should never be forgotten.

Whether you hold religious beliefs or not, there are angels along the way. People and small events which provide sign-posts for the path ahead, or sometimes simply carry you when you did not even notice you have fallen. These are the gifts of the life we still have. Take them and be grateful for each and every one of them. In an imperfect world they are a reminder that even in the face of loss, love is still possible and comes in many different guises.

This chapter which covers the first 12 months of my life after the death of my husband provides a glimpse of how the process gradually unfolded for me from one of raw grief, to unwilling acceptance and finally the ability to look forward and believe a future is possible. I hope it may be of use to others, when they too feel entirely alone, to know that alt-hough this journey begins unwanted and with an unknown destination, it is not only the landscape that changes along the way.

When I Die

Poem written by my late husband, found after his death:

When I die
Do not cry
I have gone back
From where I came
To the world of colour
Which you see every day
Without knowing I am there.
Look into the sky
Be it day or night
And there I am.

See the cloudless blue sky
Far, far away
Then stay awhile
’cause there I am.
See the clouds wandering by
A rushing helter-skelter
To nowhere, and I am with them.

Look, and see the pictures I'm painting,
Pictures you will recognise, bye and bye.
See the trees move with the wind
And watch the leaves bounce with glee
Feel the breeze upon your face
Kissing yours as we embrace.

When out at night
When all seems dark
Look closely and you'll see
The colour of the dark,
Its all-encompassing love
And I'll be there.

In fact, I'll be there
Everywhere you go,
Even when you do not
Need me anymore.

So do not cry
We met, we loved,
Laughed, we saw
The wonders of nature's beauty.
So as long as nature is there
I will still be there,
In every flower, leaf, piece of grass
In every ripple of the waves,
Drop of rain.
In every day
I'll still be there.
I have loved life.

I have loved nature
In all its glory.
I have loved the sea
The trees, flowers,
Grass and the hours.
But, more importantly
I have loved you,
And wherever I may be
I'll still love you.

Found amongst Peter's personal belongings at the Hospice, where he died August 18th, 2013.

Letters

21st August 2013

My Darling,

It is now 3 days since you died and with each hour, I feel you moving further away from me. Is it true that the soul lingers for 3 days before it starts its journey? You will know the answer now, and I feel this is right.

Your last 7 days were tortured ones, and if there is such a thing as hell, we shared it with you in your passage from this world to the next. Your final passing was quiet, in sharp contrast to the agitation and distress you showed a few days before. I hope you died in the knowledge of what was true and not the fears conjured in the mind by morphine and dying.

The boys found a poem in your notebook when we collected your belongings which they thought you had written for me. Parts of it sounded familiar, but perhaps that was just your love of Christina Rosetti and Rupert Brooke's poems influencing your own. I feel it was for me, but I am going to share it at your funeral service because I want this service to be one of love. The last verse I have kept just for me.

You will be surprised at the efforts I have gone to, to try to honour your wishes and allay your fears. I know that after your experience at sea as a young man in the navy, you did not want to be shut in a wooden box, so we have found a coffin for you made of sea grass with rope handles; you will lie in the St Erasmus Chapel of the Cathedral the night before your funeral, where we had the blessing after our civil marriage ceremony. Max has found a white ensign to be draped over your coffin, and I have scoured all the places I can think of from the Rector of Liverpool, the Lt Commander of HMS Eaglet, the local sea cadet training officer to the Salvation Army, to find a bugler to play the Last Post, so far without success. Forgive me if you have to take your leave without this. I will keep trying as long as I can, but it needs to be well done, or better not done at all.

I have chosen the *Libera me domine* from Fauré's Requiem to begin the service as it seems to echo your final struggle to leave this world, and my prayer to free you from your last suffering. Many of the readings follow the theme of the sea and of love. Stewart has offered to direct the music and many of the singers are people who have known you who are offering their skills free; some feel they will be too upset to sing.

You would not believe the number of letters and emails already. All follow the theme of laughter, love of life and you being a mentor to them.

There are moments in each day when I feel part of my heart is being squeezed so I cannot breathe. I hate the feeling of you moving further away from me, but amongst life's hard lessons, I remember something similar in the first days and weeks after my father died, as if he needed to find his place before I could find him again inside my heart. I had a vision of him then speeding through green valleys on a journey only he could travel, and then one day it was as if a voice said to me, "do not think that because you cannot see me, I am no longer there". I hope this feeling of parting is the same and when you find your place of rest, we can be at peace again.

31st August

Your funeral and cremation took place on Tuesday this week. It was a beautiful service, and I think you would have enjoyed it, even if it didn't contain Colonel Bogey at the end! Alex and Stewart brought together a wonderful choir who really did "raise the roof", with anthems by Samuel Wesley, John Ireland, Stanford's Nunc Dimittis and the Roger Fisher chant. I did find your bugler for The Last Post through the Salvation Army. I had feared that the music would be my undoing on the day but found instead that it buoyed me up and carried me through most of the service. You did look splendid draped in the white ensign and would have been surprised to see that colleagues drove all the way from the Netherlands, Spain and Finland to wish you farewell. The organist produced a great improvised rendering of *Blaze Away* at the end, which almost made up for the lack of Colonel Bogey. The funeral director walked ahead of the cortège as you started on your final journey from the Cathedral to the crematorium, and you would have loved the fact that you stopped all the traffic in city in the middle of the day – "finally cracked it, love" – I can hear you say.

The passage of days does not make it any easier to be without you. I have this overwhelming feeling of homesickness completed by the knowledge that I will never go "home" again because you are not home with me. I feel as if someone has placed a huge weight in my heart, which although I breathe, there is not enough air. It must be rather like your final months when your heart could not pump enough. Reminders of you are everywhere but you are nowhere, and this absence of you is for ever. You are there not just in things but in thoughts and conversations we can never have.

Today I drove to the coast, did our usual Saturday morning things but wanted to buy a tie for you in the tie shop, thought about the mobility scooter I dissuaded you from buying because I thought you would not manage it alone, and thought how selfish I was. I drove to the West shore where only last summer you were able to stand and look at the sea while I climbed the hill above, and I walked and then kicked off my shoes and ran towards the sea. I found I was crying with the lack of you and didn't really care if anyone could see. The sun was shining and there were small white horses which you would have loved. I thought about your poem and tried to find your pictures in the clouds, but I know that it is too soon for me to find you in another place. I paddled my feet in the sea and a few moments felt the sea draw me towards it, so much easier to let you draw me to you then to stay here alone.

Having been strong while you were ill to the point that you seemed to question my lasting love for you, the grief that I feel now seems to have unlocked so many grieves and insecurities from the past, I thought long overcome. I feel so small without you and although my head knows I am capable my heart feels totally bereft. All the things I have accomplished seem like an act which has vanished as the curtain between us has been dropped like a cruel conjuror's trick. So much of what I have done has been "because you were there".

Just as you wrote a poem for me in the last few weeks, I had one in my head, which there was never time to write in the last months because there was so much to do simply to cope. Had I written it, it would have been called, *Because you are there.* I am sorry that I did not write it in time for you. You seemed to be afraid that I did not love you enough any-more. Maybe I should try now – maybe it is never too late.

All the conversations and business of people around me seem like the trivia of a dream. I seem to be inside a bubble of aloneness where all that matters is to unravel the mystery of life and death. All through your months of illness, I was constantly surprised that I did not feel lonely, even though there were many days and nights spent alone, and I thought I was better prepared to face what was to come. I was able to appreciate all the small things – the roses in the garden, the peace and enclosure of the garden, the hills in the distance and the sky; waking up to find the sun shining through the curtains – I thought God was taking care of me. I now know it was simply because you were still here. I can still see the beauty of all those things, but I do not feel them. I feel like a well of misery in a world that is passing me by. I just want you back.

14th September

The time between writing to you is getting a little longer as the intensity of losing you recedes for short periods of time, usually as long as I am busy, and I have been at work every day last week. Evenings and weekends are a different matter as the house feels like an empty space without you. You used to say much the same thing when I had been at work or away for a night. It is just that for me this stretches out ahead for as long as I can see, a well of loneliness without you.

On the outside I look as if I am doing all right: back at work, taking on new lecture commitments and laughing and joking with people, but inside me is this gnawing emptiness and longing, like hunger, which cannot be satiated. I feel as if I have left the house and forgotten a part of myself as I shut the door.

Today I drove to the coast again. Llandudno was fine but when I went to Conwy, I could "see" you walking down the main street. I could feel you as you used to look at different times in our life together but you were not with me. Then, it takes only small things to make me cry – a driver hooting at me – and there is this overwhelming sense that there is no one beside me who is on my side; the feeling of not being special to anyone anymore, of having no safe arms to come home to. How self-centred of me; how self-indulgent when you loved life and no longer have it, while I still do. I should treasure every day as a gift, and some of the time I do. Some days I do wake up with energy, feeling excited about what I have to do in the day ahead, but then there is this huge hole inside me which carries a weight which drags me down.

I feel afraid. Afraid of not being able to live with missing you; afraid that I am not really as good at things as I believed when you were here; afraid of simply being and that being going on for years and years without you.

We knew this would happen one day, and we had plenty of time to prepare for it in the last two years, but I have been afraid of it for so long that now it has happened, I realise my fear before was but a shadow of what was to come.

How can I explain that we spoke a language that no one else fully understood? That when I talk to others, I feel as if I am speaking in a foreign language and I cannot find the words to express who I am. I can't get my head around the fact that our life is no longer relevant to anyone else. They are all moving on but "our" life is what holds me together and makes me who I am. Holding on to it is like holding a guilty secret, an addiction, which no one else must see, in case they see that I am not really the same as them but want to keep my heart with you.

I think I must have loved you very much. I cannot explain to anyone else why – simply that I did and still do.

26th November 2013

My Darling

It has been a couple of months since I had the time and the motivation to write, not because I have not missed you every moment of every day, but because I have been struggling to build some sort of life without you.

Work, which has been both my blessing and my demon, has overtaken me in the last month. November, as you knew, I always filled with teaching commitments as I hate the dark, damp and dreary days of November, and this year been a matter of sheer determination to survive. We had arranged a two-week international training course, part of which was to be taught by staff while I saw families in London for two days. A close family member of staff became terminally ill in the week prior to commencement of the course, meaning that we had to cover training and the London clinic with no days off to recover in between. I was exhausted by the end of the first week, unwell during the visit to London with two days left to teach on my return. It made me decide I cannot carry on like this in the future, and something has to be changed. This is the first step towards building a different life. I just haven't worked out "how" yet.

There was one moment you would have enjoyed – as a result of the usual practice room not being available on the day, a former patient had suggested the use of a room in Harley Street. I did skip with a small frisson of excitement a few steps down Marylebone Road as I walked back to the hotel afterwards, thinking how thrilled you would be that what you began had a momentary place in Harley Street and how astonished my mother would have been if she could have seen me there!

The following week was the meeting with medical directors, care quality commissioning directors, nursing leaders and your GP to discuss the story of your journey through the travesty of the so-called system of "care in the community". A few weeks after you died, I had sent the story to all and sundry in authority and involved in any way in your medical care as the "human story". I had prefaced it with the statement,

"This is not a complaint and should not be treated as such. It is intended to inform all agencies involved in my late husband's care of the failings in the services provided in the hope that these will be improved in the future."

The person involved in facilitating the meeting spent some time with me earlier in the week discussing the best format for the meeting, and we decided that I would present examples of failings at each level of care: Hospital, Community, Primary and Integration, describe how those incidents felt, and then how the experience could have been improved. As you can imagine, I spent a lot of time preparing for it and tackled it as if I was leading a professional meeting, as I did not want the story to be dismissed as a silly widow venting her emotions on the professionals who had tried to help you. I was given thirty minutes to talk before the meeting was opened for general discussion. Two minutes before I started, my heart started to beat so slowly and loudly that I was torn between being relieved a cardiologist was sitting on the other side of the table and hoping I might just join you at that moment.

The meeting went well, continuing beyond the hour and a half set aside for it, and your GP stayed on for over an hour to talk with me after others had left. I explained that from the patient perspective, there was no one acting as your advocate; we simply romped from one emergency crisis to another. After I had finished, the deputy executive director said that we did not have a series of crises, we had crises created for us by the system. Several important immediate changes were suggested:

- change of emphasis from task orientation amongst medical professionals to patient oriented at every level of care
- change of attitude from "can't do" to what can be done
- district nursing cover throughout the 24 period with no excuses about "hand over" periods; the same concerns could be applied to shift hand over times on the wards
- stopping use of answer machines only picked up at set times in the day
- possible setting up of a continence clinic to deal with blocked catheters at any time
- installing a system whereby hospital electronic notes alert consultants of conditions being treated by other departments within the hospital
- mandatory access to community matron to coordinate care for patients with long term chronic conditions

- review of policy of administration of enemas in the community

If even some of these are implemented, I hope it will mean that other people in the future do not have to endure some of the awful things that you went through the last couple of years.

I found it very difficult to do but had a feeling of peace and achievement when I came home afterwards. I think you would have been very proud of me, and perhaps you were there with me all the time.

Last weekend was Anna's Christening, so all the family were here at different times. It was lovely to see them all, but I did feel bereft after they had left. I am so conscious of not wanting to sap the energy they need to build their lives. I can wave them goodbye with a smile on my face but then sit on stairs and weep. It made me realise that I have already become partly accustomed to being alone here every day, but the feeling of aloneness after they had gone was penetrating. I think it is the knowledge that there is no one special who cares for me anymore – not in the sense of being wrapped up in cotton wool – but in the sense of knowing that you were always there to be care about what happened to me and what I felt, even if you did not agree with it, and could not change it. All of life had meaning <u>because you were there.</u>

This week, Joanna scanned in a series of photos of you and covers of the books you had written from the 1960s until a couple of years ago, which she put together as a slide show accompanied by Gerald Finzi's beautiful Eclogue for piano and strings playing in the background, to put up at Supervision before the day begins. I felt that those attending should be reminded that without you, none of us would be there. I may have to leave the room while it plays, because it makes me cry as soon as I see the combination of your face and the music. As I went through it in the office today to prepare myself for it, I was poignantly reminded of how you were so much more than those images to me. I miss your touch, the bigness of your hugs, the being "as one" in mind and body, how we seemed to have known each other long before we met, so that when I first saw you, I knew you. Yours was the face I had been searching for all my life.

I found another of your handwritten poems in the top drawer of your desk a couple of weeks ago.

This last month has brought me closer to making some decisions (you know how I prevaricate over these before I actually **do** anything). Without you beside me, I no longer feel as emotionally attached to work and want to start a process of getting it ready to pass on. I will still need to work, and hope I will continue to work with children, lecture when invited and more importantly, write. I don't know how to do this as the business seems to have grown into a monster which is too big for me to control. This week, the response of practitioners in Germany to the decisions we reached at the National Directors' meeting in June has started to filter in. It could best be described as revolution leading to possible devolution as the set up in Germany has hitherto been less regulated than here or in other countries. I hope we can reach a resolution but no longer feel so personally involved in what may or may not happen.

15th December 2013

My Darling

What a turbulent few weeks this has been.

On the first morning of the supervision days, an email arrived from Germany saying that one of the professors due to present at the forthcoming international conference had withdrawn after seeing the obituary in which the history of some or your political associations in the 1950s were mentioned in sensational terms. This had led them to follow a Google trail which makes links and associations, which could be true, but equally by association, may look worse than they were. It was suggested that the conference should be cancelled immediately. These particular subjects you never discussed with me, so I have no way now of either confirming or refuting the truth. The internet is a vicious tool, presenting "facts" without context, associations with no rigorous historical trail.

I have had to issue statements, both personal and public, stating that I would never have shared these particular views (many of which are now alleged to have been held by you before I was born) and that the organisation you founded and we developed together is an a-political organisation, which does not reflect or support any political, ideological, religious, social or other views of its members or former members. I also wrote to all the national heads of the organisation, suggesting that although I had no problem disassociating myself and the organisation from these views, as your widow and co-developer of the organisation which you started, I could not oversee expunging your name as the originator of the method. In view of this, if necessary, I was prepared to resign as the international head. As you can imagine, these were agonising days for me.

Recently messages of support have trickled in from heads all over the world, and I have been overwhelmed by their kindness in supporting me, stating that views alleged to have been held by you long before the organisation was founded are not relevant to today and describing you as the man I knew in all our years together. You would be very touched by what some have said. I also read in one history book that you were viewed by some of the group in the 1950s as "an adventurer", and I think this was probably right.

In the midst of this, I did book two nights at the country house hotel we had always meant to go to, but by the time we were ready to go, you were too ill for it to be a break, so we never went. It was lovely and provided me with space to rest and to get ready to edit the first of your last two books (this I read and corrected over dinner each night), but in every place I went, there was the awful absence of you. The places we have loved – Treffyn – I even started to climb a short distance up the steeper face until it occurred to me no one knew I was there, and I am so clumsy with my eyesight now that I would quite easily trip. The weather was beautiful and as I stood on the west shore – dressed in a ridiculous combination of long tweed coat and flowery Wellingtons – I tried to follow the last shaft of sunlight on the water, seeing it as a fragment of your love of life, the pathway between you and me. I willed the sunbeam along the water to wash up to my feet with each wave, not knowing if the tide was on the ebb or flood, hoping that the water would find me and this would be a confirmation of your embrace, that each wave that reached me would enfold me in the only touch, the only form of blessing we can share now.

In this wonderful landscape, surrounded by all the beauty of the earth, I still feel as if I am in the midst of death, as if death not only surrounds me but is more real than life. I feel detached from the real world; time has no real meaning, and as I realise that it is now nearly four months since you died, it could be only yesterday. I sleep, but do not seem to know it; I dream, and you often visit my dreams, although I rarely remember more than a passing impression in the morning. I go through the motions of daily living, making appointments and plans but with no real sense of what anything is *for*, just filling time.

I ordered a copy of CS Lewis', *A Grief Observed* and was surprised to see him begin, "no one told me that grief feels so like fear". This is exactly how it feels. He also describes a sense of unreality, wondering if his whole marriage was but a dream, and as the dream passes, he returns to his former self, as if his marriage was just a holiday or interlude in the flow of life. Then he questions whether life is also a dream, a sort of awful illusion. I feel that too. I remember asking, no arguing with you, about the meaning of life in an existential sense, and me saying,

"I know that it sounds very egotistical, but as a child I used to wonder how the world could continue to be if I was no longer here to observe it."

You said, "But of course the world is here, and would continue to be if you or I were not."

And I said, "Yes, logically I know that, but I also know that the world as I know it is a projection of my senses. What happens when the senses can no longer feel and the mind perceive it? Is it all an illusion, a warped perspective seen from a very particular point of view?"

I feel that you still exist, even though I know your body was incinerated to a pile of ashes. I still feel that you exist whole and in the flesh. Soon after you died, you came to me in a dream and stood just out of reach. In my dream, I even remonstrated with you, saying that 'you could not still be there as you appeared, I knew you were a pile of ashes', and you insisted, 'but I *am* here'.

I do not begin to understand what it is all about or the purpose of it all. I think Plato was partly right, that all things are composed of atoms, and living things are held together by an energy force (magnetism?). The laws of physics tell us that energy is never lost, and therefore when the life energy which holds living things together dies, that energy must go somewhere – the Christian concept of the soul. The physical world also suggests that it cannot remain intact but must scatter – and yet I feel that you are still whole – that your energy is still held together by you, that you are still somehow with me but apart from me.

Death seems all pervading; it fills my time and grief is such a demanding master, sapping me of energy, of the life force I need to live and to be connected to life. Is this what Freud meant by libido? I do not resent it, but I do feel consumed by it and my intellect tells me it is an indulgence to allow it to hold me quite so resolutely in its grasp.

CS Lewis said that grief prevented him from seeing God. As long as he held on to his grief, it prevented God from finding him. I do not feel like that, but I do feel removed, very small and full of fear. Perhaps that is just different words for the same thing. You knew how much fear ate into my life, and it was only during our years together that I felt stronger than the fear and occasionally knew glimpses of that elusive thing other people refer to as, “faith”. As I grew in courage, so I started to understand that fear and faith are antagonists – fear prevents us from being able to believe that somehow everything will be all right – in the words of Mother Julian of Norwich, that “all shall be well and all manner of things shall be well”. Faith allows us to face the future and contemplate the possibility of fear but to feel that somehow, we will be equipped to deal with it. I wish I could find that place again. Not in the religious sense, but in the living sense you gave me the armour of faith, but it seemed to slip away with you, and it drifts further away with time.

I spend a great deal of time alone now, not always lonely, but definitely alone. It bothers me that this aloneness does not always bother me as much as it should. I can lose myself in this: in writing, in thinking, in listening to music, which has been my constant companion in these last months. I fear I could become a recluse away from work, and wither away unseen, a façade that functions on the outside but is shrinking within.

It is now the third Sunday in Advent. As I struggle once again to understand the meaning of Christmas (so simple when a small child) and I loathe how cheap and tawdry it has become, as if it is a ghastly parody of itself – another illusion – I try again to understand the meaning of “the Word”. I understand the light coming into darkness – the fear of darkness coming of it being nothing or no-thingness – a state with no physical reference point and the light shining like a beacon. I think that the “Word” is life and love, that positive energy that “is”, but wants and seeks nothing for itself other than more of the same. In this modern, ugly world, I wonder how this can “be”. None of the fripperies of Christmas seem important –

neither the presents nor the feasting. All that seems to matter is that you are not here. You are my Christmas.

12th January 2014

A new year and I cannot understand how this can be the first year since we met that I continue to be and life will continue without you sharing it. The world will turn and with each moment "we" are forgotten by the world around. Other lives are lived, hopes projected for the future and our lost world is of no significance. The longer minutes of daylight each day help, and I do experience longer patches when I "am" without feeling quite so lost, and yet much of my "now" still feels unreal. Much of the time it is as if my waking life is my dream. I do not really remember going to sleep each night, although I know I remember you every night before I fall asleep and wish you there beside me.

I seem to have done quite a lot since you died, and yet none of it seems to register. It is as if I am waiting. I know you cannot come back, and yet I am waiting for something…just around the corner, just over the horizon, tomorrow, next month, next year, a whisper, a touch – I don't know what it is I am waiting for – I wish it was you. It is like listening for a sound which is just beyond earshot, the view over the crest of a hill, just beyond vision. Is this the invisible veil that separates this life from the next?

You would laugh if you could see the hermit's life I lead. I am not sure a nun could be more chaste or more contemplative in the long silent spaces, which is my life. I try not to look much beyond tomorrow, because if I thought this was going to be the next thirty years, I could not bear it, and yet I am not unhappy all of the time. I can appreciate the bright sunny days when they happen and like my father, make a conscious decision to make the most of each and every one of them. Music is my salvation and seems literally, to speak, not only to, but for my soul. I am so grateful to whatever it was in my childhood that gave me this gift of music, a language so much more eloquent than words.

Christmas came and went with the children making it nearly normal. William, Sarah and Freddy arrived on the 20th and with them here, meals to cook, things to tidy, I had a "role" again and felt almost real, nearly normal. When I awoke on Christmas morning, someone had hung a huge stocking on my bedroom door – the first since you and I had our first Christmas together – I felt extraordinarily touched and blessed to have this family we raised together and the partners they have chosen. We all went to Christopher and Mary's for the day, and the day was all right, but the Cathedral service was a very strange experience – a kaleidoscope of the all the different times of my and our life good and bad – brought together. In one aisle were the boys, their wives and two grandchildren, with me and the children's father beside me. Except for Patricia, this was my family before you and me, in the place where we had our blessing, where we raised the children in the years when they were choristers, and where the image of you lying in the St Erasmus Chapel and of your funeral is still penetratingly present. The singing was amazing. We could have been a small choir of our own, and yet this was not my "before" family anymore, because in between, there was you, you and me, and the life that shaped me into who I am now. I can never be the same again.

I have started to look at houses. I don't know if I want to move, although the area becomes rougher each month and parking is a daily problem. I am starting to clear things out – not "throwing away" as I know you feared I might – but just as you liked to collect things, I cannot think clearly or see beyond where I am while there is clutter. I need to pare away the things I do not need. In my need to create external order from my inner chaos, home is beginning to look obscenely tidy, and I will paint anything that does not move! Small things seem to upset me very easily, and I seem to struggle with the most mundane of daily chores, although I have done them for years. It does not take much to catapult me into temporary meltdown.

Oh Darling, you are an impossible act to follow. How can anyone ever fill the space you have left behind, and can I ever let anyone else in? I look at this ageing self with wrinkles deepening, flesh sagging, this once-so-desired and insatiable but now unloved body and wonder how it can ever sing again.

You knew more than anyone that the only way I ever became truly close was through my body, that despite my ability to write (and much to my own surprise, later on, to speak), it is touch which has always spoken for me, probably the reason why the people who are closest to me are those I have had closest physical contact with: you and my children. Without that physical closeness, I feel isolated, a thing apart from the world around me, and I find myself becoming more protective of it every day, like a young adolescent fearful of their first encounter.

10th February 2014

Darling

This week I am not doing so well. I seem to have shrunk, as if to diminish the empty hole within. While there have been many good things in recent weeks, in the last 10 days, they feel as if as they have been only bad, and without you beside me, without you to come home to, I do not seem to have the resilience to withstand them. Today I have cried – a lot – knowing with certainty that you will never be here again to help me with these things; that you can never be there, by my side again.

The legacy of our work brings new problems with it every day, and I feel overwhelmed by them questioning how many of them are of my own creation whilst with others I feel angry and impotent that problems have been fashioned by the failures, ambition, ignorance or arrogance of others. I want to put things right and can hear you saying, "some people will always dislike you, even those who don't know you, because they think you stand in the way of what they want". I know this is true of many of the problems I am dealing with now. I want to "do the right thing", but so often that seems to be surrendering what you and I have built so that others can have their way, whether they deserve it or not. I feel ragged and overwhelmed by such responsibility. I simply want to come home to a place where you and I are and can make believe that the rest of the world does not matter so long as we are. But this wish is of yesterday. It cannot be again. I thought I was beginning to move forward, but today the lack of you is a strong as the moment I knew you had died, that there was no going back, no ability to change anything ever again, that it was ended.

Good things in the last few weeks: Participation in a BBC radio prime time programme, which went OK. You would have been proud of me; I was proud of me and in a different sense from before! I simply felt I had done an adequate job –

no huge fear before or elation afterwards – just a job done well enough; invitation to join a new project, which may give me the lead outside this maelstrom, which I struggle to deal with every day. I will wait to find out more; possible new research project based on the school programme – in London this week to discuss. I have made a start on editing your first book and must return to this so that my energy is on positive projects, not the endless defence and tidying up of where we have been; invitations to lecture or teach abroad, which when they arrive, I think, *I can do that*, but then the daily grind begins, and I think, *How can I do that? Where will I find the energy? Where will I find the inner resources?*

With all that we have done, I feel I should not have to worry about, how will I work? How will I support myself in the years to come? But I have learned life does not come on a plate. I wish I had the leap of faith to be able to say I am going to stop all the things that exhaust me, throw them overboard with reckless abandon and simply have faith in the future, but I fear there will be nothing to sustain me in their place. Even as I write this, I hear the contradiction. How can something destroy and sustain me at the same time?

Darling, there is no replacement for you. While I occasionally look around, I see nothing that I would want, and neither do I want to let go of you to make room for someone new, because they will not, they cannot be you.

I hope you are in a better place where all the dreams and longings of your life here are fulfilled. I hope too that there will be space for me with you again one day. Darling, I miss you.

15th March 2014

My Darling

This all seems so unreal. For a few days I think I am doing better and then I realise, that somewhere, I am just waiting for you to come back, and yet I know that you never can and you never will. This is my life now. You have given me all you could, and you have shaped me into who I am, but the absence of you is everywhere and at times I still feel abject without you.

I miss the conversation (God knows what we talked about all the time, but talk we did), the "knowing", the sense of belonging and knowing that I was loved. The latter is within me but is not yet with me, and I feel so alone for the lack of it. The worst thing about widowhood, and nobody talks about it, is the total isolation which comes with it. For months now I have felt as if I live inside a bubble simply looking at the rest of the world.

My life is one of extraordinary contrasts. Last week, I presented at a conference in London which generated articles in two of the nationals with me as the lead and was followed up with three BBC radio interviews before catching the train home. I knew it was a job well done and as I do more alone, I am gradually starting to see what you used to tell me but which I could never see for myself – I am good at this – and I have earned my place in my own right. I realised this week that I had been the moon to your star for a long time. I was happy for that to be, never having the confidence to believe I could perform at this level alone, and now I find I can and think you would be very proud if you could see. Then, I step out at the train station to total obscurity. When I come home, it is as if I cease to exist. How it is possible that I exist on these two levels?

I have also realised that if I am ever to make a life for myself for the life I have left, somehow, I have to let you go. I wish I could find you inside myself as I did with my father a few weeks after he died, but we have not reached that stage yet. For a little while last week, I thought I felt you beside me saying, "if you have the courage to go out and live again, to find joy, love and laughter, I will come with you; I will be beside you, you will not lose me", but I fear just that. That, if I embrace life, take emotional risks somehow, I will lose you, or/and the love and respect of my children for not seeming to preserve you. I leap between the extremes of thinking I can do things and then the total isolation of now.

How does one do this?

2nd June 2014

My Darling,

Where do I begin, or do I need to, because I feel that you already know and are with me in whatever I do? This is a good feeling, which I want to hold on to – forever – if we can.

As spring arrived and I became more and more aware of the loneliness and isolation of my existence since you died, I decided that I could no longer justify feeling sorry for myself unless I took a step to do something about it. It is all very well people saying 'develop a circle of friends', 'enjoy the company of your female friends' – this I do, and I value – but this is not the same as belonging with someone, of sharing not only company but a full emotional, physical and intellectual life with someone. I have missed this desperately. No one can ever replace you, but I would like to live a fuller life again, have someone to care for and be loved in return.

So, after a telephone conversation with Patricia one evening, in which I repeated the now regular pattern of going to work and spending the evenings and weekends alone, I signed up to an internet dating site, feeling both guilty and mortified that I needed to do this. You would have laughed like a drain if you could have seen me in the evenings, trawling through the hundreds of possibilities, (if you have the time to do it), clucking to myself, "oh dear, oh dear", "oh dear, no, you need deleting", until occasionally something remotely possible would turn up. It took a few weeks before I had the courage to start to list a few as "favourites", horrified at the idea of having to follow it up or even worse, if one of them contacted me! Gradually, a small queue of those interested began to form in my "favourites" folder and the process of exchanging emails began. One, who immediately was a good intellectual sparring partner but who carried so much baggage and seemed to live such a complicated life that I dismissed him as a future prospect, but one who would probably make a good friend if we ever meet. Another, probably a "sound" prospect, living fairly close, but clearly not passionate or interested enough to follow up; then an artist, with a face I seemed to recognise and a past which sounded similar but different to yours. He called, and for two weeks, we talked every night on the 'phone, until I felt we had established a rapport. There were many reservations, but there was a pull and so, due to join Rosie, Gerard and family for a few nights of their holiday in the Lakes, I suggested we meet for coffee and possibly lunch en route to join them.

It was a surprising meeting of opposites, awkward to begin with, not unpleasant, but not quite comfortable either. The strangest thing was to walk arm in arm with someone else. I have not done that in more than twenty-seven years. There was a physical attraction and this surprised and derailed me. I had not expected it, and it seemed to be mutual. This very quickly became a driving force and in an alarmingly short period of time we arranged for him to visit me at the weekend. I felt excited and happy at the prospect, for the first time in many, many months (or is it years?)

It was a beautiful sunny day as I did my usual Saturday things, and a few hours before he was due to arrive a text message came through from your son saying that today (of all days) he had waded into the sea on an ebbing tide to let your ashes go. I did not know if this was a gift from you to me, to say that until we meet again, I am free to make a life for myself, or, if it was a protest that I was in any way seeking to replace you. You should know that you can never be replaced. No one can ever be you to me, or me to you, but I do know that the capacity to love is neither finite nor small, and in being willing to love again, it does not lessen what we had and what is gradually becoming a part of who I am.

Having spent some time together now, I fear that this new relationship has potential stumbling blocks. In a funny way, I feel you are with me in it, gently urging me on, to discover and enjoy aspects, which enables me to see that life is still here for me, while recognising that the mixture could be flawed. I fear that it will end in tears – yet – it is wonderful to have companionship again; someone I feel at home with; someone to talk to on the phone at the end of every day with whom increasingly I am able to talk about almost anything; to have plans for the weekend ahead; to feel just a little bit loved; but there is also the barb in the tail; seeing the differences between us and wondering if they can be worked through.

I am grateful that you seem to be with me in this and some of what this man has to offer carries the essence of you, although vitally, he is also very different from you. Are the points of similarity you gently blowing like a breeze to push me in the right direction, to set me on a course, though the final destination is not known? I feel this, as if the colours and the energy you wrote about have merged with the colours of his paintings, that there is no competition between you and that it is all right to visit places we knew but also to plan new horizons. This man is not you; there is no reason why he should be and gradually this relationship seems to be forming its own path.

He met with the family last weekend, a brave and probably premature step. William, Sarah and Freddy had been here for a week of their holiday. It was the first time that the whole family have been together at home since your funeral, now seven round the table and three children sleeping upstairs – how has this small house been able to accommodate a family that has doubled in size? Both William and Patricia were quite distressed by the reality of being here together and recognising the absence of you. Adding another man probably made it worse, but I do not want to have secrets from them. All is so complicated as I try to navigate my way through this sea of change without a compass and until recently, under a clouded sky.

24th June 2014

My Darling

What a difference a few weeks makes. Despite the differences I wrote about in my last letter, this relationship is still going and seems to be developing a depth and closeness much of the time, which I am struggling to believe and come to terms with.

I find myself questioning, am I deluding myself? Is it just a salve for months of loneliness? Is it just the pull of physical love after so many years or am I "playing" at having someone love me again? It may be a little of all these things, but it feels more. It seems to have taken on a force of its own, which feels as if it is being driven from elsewhere. There is a closeness, a concern for each other and a desire to mould (not change) to fit one another better. In the first couple of weeks when I wondered if I should end it before it began, I could not believe the feelings of abject loneliness which descended with the prospect of returning to the dark place I had lived in for the last nine months, where time had no meaning and I cannot seem to remember its passing or what I had done. No one can replace you or the life that we had, in which we shared everything – each other, home, family and work – all merged into one life, so that when you died, I no longer knew where one part of life ended and the other began. Now I am beginning to see that it is possible to have aspects of life again, without them all having to be in the same pot.

William was very distressed when they were staying here for a week of their holiday, probably not helped by introducing another man into the family and also for him being here for the first time with time to spare and places to visit where you used to be. I know one of the hardest things for me in the months after you died was going to places for the first time where we had always been together. I could see you, feel you, hear you in each and every one of them, and the absence of you hurt so much, I could hardly bear it. Bit by bit I have learned to do it, and the second time is easier, but for him, I think as long as he was away and working it was as if things were almost the same and the realisation that home can never be the same again was very painful for him.

I have tried to explain that no one else can ever replace you; that I have come to learn that after death all we are left with, and the only thing no one can take away from us, is the love that we shared; that is there forever. We have an infinite capacity to love and love begets love; that before each of the children were born I could not believe that I would have love to spare for another, and yet when another one was born that love was all encompassing; that life as we go forward is similar – we have choice – choice to take risks, never forgetting what we had, but taking it on into new relationships and a new phase of life as people who have grown as a result of the love that we have had and the love we have shared. Given the choice to love again or be "safe" and alone, why would we choose to live without the former?

I have spent so many months asking what was the point of me without you? It wasn't only as if I did not exist other than just treading water, I seemed to have no purpose other than filling time.

I took a leaf out of my father's book after my mother died and have aimed to be joyful when with others, and not to spread my sense of desolation. But at times I have had to give myself a stern "talking to", consciously remembering the children and the grandchildren and reminding myself, that although they do not need me as they used to do, that without me those six (and growing number) of lives could not be; that I have a purpose not just in who and where I am now or in what I do, but in the things that I have done that will (hopefully) exist long after me.

This new man (and yes, he has a name, but this is someone else's story and does not belong here), has made me feel that I do have purpose and value again for who and where I am now, that I exist in the real world again and not in a bubble removed and floating like flotsam somewhere detached from real existence. I have started to want things again, to aim for some things and to change others; to have hopes for the future and to care for and about him.

I can visit places with him we used to go, still with some nostalgia but gladness for how beautiful they are rather than sorrow and a sense of total isolation as if the place, and I existed apart from the rest of the world. As we sat at the top of one of the Welsh mountain passes on a sunny June evening, it felt like a touch of paradise and as if your world and ours met not in collision but in celebration.

I want to be free to work under my own name, to take the enormous risk of having faith in myself for the future but knowing that part of this is the thought of having someone else beside me. I am mindful of not wanting to hurt others by seeking comfort and reassurance for myself from their love and trust. I feel very confused in this new place, glad for it but fearful of being selfish and creating a false illusion that has taken some of the pain away.

1st July 2014.

My Darling

How my moods seem to shift and career from one extreme to the other. Tonight I am very, very tired and have felt quite unwell all day, I think from sheer exhaustion.

This has been a month of travel and presentations all over the south of England – a good idea when arranged in the winter months when all ahead looked empty – but not so clever now. I returned from a presentation in Surrey on Sunday (down on Saturday, presentation in the afternoon, travel home on Sunday morning with 4 train changes each way) to be met by new man. We had a lovely two days, walking in the mountains on Monday on a rare, perfect, sunny June day. The scenery was superb, and if there are places and times where heaven and earth meet, this was one of them. I think you were there too, not to interfere, but to share with us. But on returning home, there are things that don't feel right, and I don't know what to do. I have felt so fragile today, physically exhausted I think, and destabilised by the things which do not "feel" right.

10th July

My Darling

Things continue to progress. While some differences persist and grow with time, an extraordinary closeness, a "oneness" has developed at others, which I never expected to feel again. It is different from the one we shared, but that is good as it feels like a new chapter in my life, which in no way diminishes or obliterates the chapters that have gone before. I am trying to take it week by week and not look into the future, but let this simply be. Whether it is a part of my journey through recovery or whether it becomes a permanent part of my recovery and my future. I do not know and cannot begin to map ahead. I am very surprised to find I can even function this way. You know how much I always wanted to know what was going to happen next!

The last month was a crazy month with 4 presentations in different parts of the south of England, returning home each time in between and more than 1500 miles covered. I have felt more exhausted than I can say at times, and despite the work, money worries have grown with all the legal bills that have had to be met in taking advice about the international situation and trying to plan a way ahead. Losing the international side would mean the loss of a significant portion of income, which I may not be in a position to jettison as easily as I would wish.

Advance copies of the new book which I wrote during my convalescence after surgery last year in those precious last few months where we were at home together while I recovered and you continued to fight to hold on to the life you loved and lived so well, arrived this week. It is a good book, and as I thumbed through it, instead of joy, I felt a sense of indignation that what you started and we developed together has been so undermined by the ambitions and ignorant self-righteousness of those who, based on limited information, think they "know" or know better.

Sarah sent a marketing brief last week for setting up a new company under my own name. I did not recognise myself! Have I really done all the things listed? When reading these things, it always seems to me that isolated incidents are blown up and presented as regular events, but even I can see that the number of books and languages in which they have been published is worth something. And yet, going to see a film with new man at the weekend – a modern "Love Story" about a young couple both with terminal cancer – reminded me that all our achievements, all the material wealth we may accumulate are as nothing in the face of death. The only traces we leave behind which are enduring are those of life (children) and love. Love lives on in the hearts of those left behind and is passed to those we love now and in the future. This is the real gift of who we are. Everything else is simply survival.

Poem found amongst my husband's papers after he died.

To You, My Wife

Darling, I thought you should know,
I never fell in love with you,
You see, I never had a need to.
I have loved you many times before we met
In the lives we have lived before.
So, when we as strangers met
I knew the day, the time
To love you yet again.
For as long as the days and years we have together,
In this, one of our many loves before and those to come.

To You, My Husband

How can I begin to tell what you have been to me?
As two people who came from different worlds,
From different generations and different times,
For many years, we were like star-crossed lovers,
Forbidden by time and convention from even dreaming to be;
And yet, the world had meaning,
Because you were there.

Yours was the face I had known all my life.
The unknown voice that had echoed through my childhood,
And when we as adults met,
The longing of the heart found speech in the language of the head.

For years, I talked to you when you were not there;
When we found and lived and shared each other
And passion found its home,
While loving you, I still did not fully understand,
That all of my life had meaning, quite simply,
Because you were there.

The days were lighter and brighter:
The dreariness of winter, the hope of spring,
The sultry days of summer,
The vibrant colours and dank decay of autumn,
Through the seasons and the years, you sustained me,
Because you were there.

You gave me the strength of a lioness,
To follow paths I did not know I wanted to take;
The tenacity of a tigress,
To persevere when I did not know where the path would lead;
You were proud of me when I could not see a reason to rejoice,
And you wanted me when I was impossible,
Simply because I was there.

When age stripped you of your strength,
With a heart grown huge from love of life,

Your lungs infused with water instead of air,
You became a gentler man.
A man for whom love was all.

In those months, there was not a day
When there was not joy in coming home to you.
Joy in visiting you.
Joy in knowing you were there.
And now, your gift to me is that Joy.
The joy of hoping that all shall be well,
Simply because you were there.

Now the years stretch out ahead,
Another life beyond the one we shared.
A small lifetime's collection of moments
That fashioned me into who I am.

But as only those who have been touched by death before can know,
You are never coming back.
My life ahead is to be lived without you.
Love carried in the heart,
Memories in the head,
A life ahead worth living,
Because you were there.

I still have choice.
To remain in the places we shared,
Or,
To embrace the possibilities and gifts that are put in my way.
Never forgetting,

But finally acknowledging,
I am still here.

God Speed, My Love.

Postscript

It is now more than 12 years since my husband died. Sometimes it feels like yesterday and at other times, it seems as if it happened in a different life to someone else.

Time and memory are fickle creatures creating distance as tangible as mileage while also summoning images and sensations that feel real and in the moment. This can be a source of comfort as well as sadness.

Seen through the passage of twelve years, I have come to realise that death leaves an indelible imprint on the souls of those who have loved. This is not a stigmata that continues to weep but a wound that heals over time, allowing the rest of the body to recover, to live beyond the empty space and to find joy in living while changing the physical and emotional structure of the self for ever. If we are lucky, the essence of the relationship we have lost becomes part of the self.

At first, we seek fragments of the lost everywhere, in the places that we went, material things, the people we knew, the stories we shared and the longing that is left behind. At some point – and the time when that point is reached is different for everyone – the nature of the seeking starts to change. Just like physical pain and recovery, the intensity of yearning slowly lessens; days become ordinary – dull even – and gradually a desire to be connected to life and others starts to grow.

Wisdom comes from unexpected sources: A taxi driver who used to drive us to the airport when we were teaching abroad who remarked, "you do not owe him life"; snippets overheard – "life has a habit of reclaiming you" – and one day a realisation that in order to do this, you have to let go. This is not to forget or to "move on" but to integrate what is best into the self and to take it forward into world. Whether you believe in reincarnation, resurrection or simply that everything ends with death, we do live on in the hearts of those we have loved.

Modern Britain is not good at recognising or supporting the dying or the bereaved.

Following two years of what I can only describe as a travesty of failures in social care and communication between services, death was like an amputation. We had experienced sixteen emergency ambulance admissions in eighteen months, a series of carers coming and going, often changing every two weeks or following re-assessment after yet another hospital admission, well-meaning but ineffectual occupational therapists who offered more equipment, which did little to help with the day-to-day care but contributed a great deal to a mountain of clutter. On one occasion when a bed lever was offered as the solution to the fact that I could not get him in and out of bed on my own, I snapped, "if you bring one more item of equipment, the equipment will be here, but I will not!" Following his final ten days of terminal hospice care, after death, there was nothing.

My children were wonderful and did everything they could in the following days and weeks, but they were at a stage in their lives where they all had very young children and could not take extensive time off from their fledgling careers. Neither would I have wanted them to. This was their time to build their family lives, and I was acutely conscious of not wanting to lean on them.

I soon discovered that death does not just bring loss in its wake but a total change to the life you had previously led. Single adults are "untidy"; they do not fit in with the former social world of couples; daily life and simple things like holiday ambitions change and so the social ground of common experience starts to shift. I knew I wanted to continue to belong to general society with a healthy mix of families, couples, single people and colleagues but the entrance to this world seemed to recede with time. I did not feel like a widow and bizarrely did not want to be viewed as such, but I could see I no longer "belonged" in aspects of my former life.

Whereas after a physical amputation there would be some after-care and rehabilitation, after death, there is none. A few months later, when working in London, I met a former colleague of the Jewish faith. When she asked me what I had done, whom I had seen, what regular support I had over the previous six months, she was appalled when I said other than going to work and seeing members of my family who lived nearby, nothing. She said that for the first twelve months following a bereavement, members of the Jewish community would have visited almost daily, bringing food, but more importantly, company to the person who was left behind. This sounded like another world to me and to other friends I know who have lost partners since.

When we had collected the death certificate from the hospice the day after he died, the nurse had quietly explained that a bereavement counselling service was available, but it could not be accessed until six weeks had passed. Having read the work of Elisabeth Kubler-Ross, a Swiss American psychiatrist and pioneer in near-death studies, intellectually, I knew what to expect and did not think counselling could help me to understand more. Twelve weeks later, I recognised that I seemed to have fallen into rather a deep well of being alone, which I did not know how to climb out of. Reluctantly, and without great expectations, I asked if I could join the waiting list, dreading that I would be assigned a counsellor who was overly sentimental, which would immediately reinforce my remaining defence mechanisms.

I was lucky. I was given a counsellor who was matter of fact and never probed too deeply. She simply allowed me to share the many practical worries that I would previously have discussed with my husband and to work out solutions. While I saw her for weekly sessions, I continued to write to him and this duet played out in different places, affected an outlet for feelings expressed in the letters and support in exploring ways to live the life remaining for me, with my counsellor.

Towards the end of the first year and with the coming of spring, encouraged by one of my children, I met my current partner. Our life together is someone else's story and would remain so, but eight years ago he was diagnosed with a life limiting illness. While we can never know what will happen next, there is a high probability that one day I may be left without him. In the light of my past experience, do I fear this? Yes. Do I think I will be able to live with the space that is left behind? I hope so. Will it be different next time? Yes, because the impact of death is exclusive to the relationship and is never the same twice. Will it be easier next time? Probably not, just different. What have I learned? That the only thing we can make a difference to is here and now; to make the best of the gifts that are put in our way and have hope and faith in whatever the future brings.

Is there more that society in the United Kingdom could do to support the dying and anyone following the death of a loved one?

Yes.

Help for the Dying

Following my husband's death, a reflective review was set up at the local hospital to discuss the many failings that had occurred in the "care in the community" that he had received. Attendees included the chief executive of the hospital, one of his consultants, head of district nursing, someone involved in patient relationships and his GP. His GP was a good man, but afterwards he confided to me that he found it really difficult to know how to treat patients for whom (in his view) he could do nothing. He said that the Medicine he had been taught was about healing and he struggled when faced with those he could not heal.

I was astonished by this and said that one of the most important parts of being a doctor or health worker was to bring relief and comfort to those who have no hope of recovery. Management of pain, support for disability and knowing that there will be adequate support at the end, can make all the difference to both the patient and the family. Our experience was of a health service driven by technology rather than physicians – a system where if the "computer says no" – the needs of the patient do not exist. Examples of this were postponement of an emergency operation because the hospital appointment had never been sent to us (return to the bottom of the list), being denied extra help at home two weeks before he died because answers to the questionnaires filled out by district nurses were two points short of the tick boxes needed to access additional care and taking two full black bin bags of over-prescribed medication to the local pharmacy following his death.

Ironically, in the years before his final illness, he had returned to a subject he had written about extensively some thirty years before – psychosomatic illness, somatogenic illness and the effects upon physical and mental health. For someone who understood the relationship between brain and body and the mind's ability to affect physical changes in the body so well, the chaos of the system designed to treat him seemed like a mockery of all that he had written.

It was in the last two weeks of his life that we were lucky to be embraced by the local hospice. How different was this experience. This was a serene place, and despite its purpose, a happy place. Here, everything that could be done to provide physical and emotional comfort was offered and more than anything else, kindness and dignity were afforded to the family.

I cannot praise too highly what this service provides, not only to patients in their final days, but growing support through a range of day care facilities and pain management to those living with life limiting illnesses. Some hospices also offer bereavement services; one offers walking groups, children's groups, WhatsApp groups, counselling, children's counselling, and the bereaved are contacted for up to three years and invited to all bereavement events and services.

This service relies heavily on donations and fund raising to carry out its essential and invaluable work. Despite this, in my view, it is the gold standard of care for the thousands of patients for whom the health service can do no more. In an ideal world, what the hospice service provides should be an exemplary division of the National Health Service.

According to a hospice staff member, "Hospices are working hard to change the social stigma surrounding them and to educate GPs on referrals and getting people to us earlier. The largest part of our work is our Day Services. So, seeing people weekly to give them physical and emotional support plus pain management, so that they can go home and be well for longer. This is the lesser known part of the hospice. But again, it's all down to funding. The more NHS funding, the more people we can get to and critically, earlier."

Supporting Bereavement

If you know someone whose close relative, friend or colleague has died:

- Be there. Pick up the phone; knock on the door.
- Do not be embarrassed about saying the wrong thing or upsetting the person. Being upset is the beginning of recovery;
- Simply listen.
- Be a companion; call at regular intervals and ask "how has your day been?" This is the part that I

missed most – simply having someone to share the day with.

- Include the person in a range of normal events.
- Let them talk about mundane worries.
- Help with small practical problems if needed. These can pile up to seem like a mountain when tackled alone.
- Continue to talk about the person who has died. The legacy of love and laughter do not end with death.
- Ensure that information about support and counselling for bereavement is available and accessible.
- Acknowledge the process of grief in the workplace and social events not just in public displays such as mass vigils following the death of someone not personally known to the crowd.
- Remind people that recovery takes time and that the duration of recovery is different for everyone. The Victorians were right to recognise a two-year period of mourning, not in wearing "widow's weeds" and being separated from society, but that vulnerability is present to a greater or lesser degrees for at least two years.

Finally, remember that birth and death are the two universally shared experiences. In the words of a song from the musical Chess, "no one in your life is with you constantly". In my case, I was lucky enough to have known him so well.